Infinity
Jacqueline James

PUBLISHED by PARABLES
Earthly Stories with a Heavenly Meaning

Poetry With A Twist
Copyright ©Jacqueline James
November, 2020

Published By Parables
December, 2020
ISBN 978-0-692-67302-7

All Rights Reserved. No part of this book may be reproduced or utilized in any form or by any means, electronic or mechanical, including photocopying, recording, or by any information storage and retrieval system, without permission in writing from the author.

Unless otherwise specified Scripture quotations are taken from the authorized version of the King James Bible.

Readers should be aware that Internet Web sites offered as citations and/or sources for further information may have been changed or disappeared between the time this was written and when it is read.

Infinity
Jacqueline James

Table of Content.

General

1. Fight or Flight...   8
2. The Golden Seniors...   9
3. The Move...   10
4. My Stuff...   12
5. Don't Run...   14
6. Pressure Bust Pipes...   15
7. Sorry...   16
8. The Plan...   17
9. Lack of Attention...   19
10. Not a "Friend"...   20
11. Be Like U...   21
12. The Best of my Night...   22
13. The "new"...   23
14. Negative Energy...   24
15. I Have Poems...   26

Spiritual

1. Only Through Jesus..   28.
2. Only God Knows...   29
3. Jesus Therapy...   30
4. Greatness in me...   31
5. You Let Your "Angel" Slip Away...   32
6. FEAR-NOT...   33
7. I'm Healed...   35
8. Holy Women...   36
9. Holy Women on One Accord...   37
10. Holy Women Working for God Promises...39
11. Holy Women Standing on the Promises of the Lord...   41

Educational
1. The President... 46
2. The Winners... 48
3. Being...Doesn't... 49
4. Provoked... 50
5. Police Brutality... 52
6. Them 2 Days... 54
7. U Can't Buy Loyalty... 55
8. 1 Million-to-Infinity... 56

Informative
1. Don't Forget 2 Love You 4 You... 60
2. Surviving the "Storm"... 62
3. Taxes... 63
4. I Love all my Imperfections... 65
5. The "Victims"... 68
6. What is a Friend... 70
7. I Trusted... 72
8. High Self-esteem... 74
9. My Girls... 75
10. Where will my soul go... 76
11. The After Mask... 77

Entertainment
1. I Had a Wang-Bang Weekend... 80
2. My Son Won't Stop Eating... 82
3. The Television-set... 84
4. Nacho cheese (Not-your-cheese) 85
5. Like "scramble-eggs"... 86
6. See "What had Happen was"! 87
7. This Phone... 89
8. I Sailed the Sea... 90
9. Water "mass"... 91

INFINITY

10. The "70's Party...   92
11. My House Guest...   94
12. Under the Shade Tree...   96
13. Falling Snow...   97

Special Dedication
1. A Special Aunt..   100
2. Final Moments...   101
3. God Called her Home...   102
4. What my Mother means to me... 104
5. A Battle for "Joy"...   105
6. Happy... Yet Sad...   107
7. Until we Meet Again...   109

About the Author

Jacqueline James is a Christian author professional writer and poetess. Jacqueline has written several books of poetry as well two children stories which includes "Happy Hauntings" and "My ABC Song" all of which has been successfully published with worldwide distribution. Jacqueline spends countless hours researching the best-case sceneries on peace and serenity through human behaviors. She then uses this knowledge alone with personal incentives to compose beautiful arrays of poetry. Jacqueline is on a personal mission to inform, inspire, and education her readers (you) as she entertains you when you soak up her words of endearment.

The Dedication

The book Infinity is dedicated to my oldest Granddaughter Angel Griffin.

Angel is a very charming free-spirited individual with excellent leadership qualities. Angel is capable of achieving any challenges put before her. She makes each struggle her own personal success story then uses it as a guide to inspire others.

Angel generates an enormous amount of energy which draws in multitudes of followers to be motivated by her persona.

I truly admire her and look forward to seeing her at the "top".

My love for my Granddaughter Angel will continue on through infinity.

Thank You

  I would like to thank God for continuously blessings me with an infinite amount of beauty to be expressed through each of my written poetry. God has blessed me with a river of words that flows with the humility of His existence in my life.
  I am forever grateful.

  Thank you Centilus Buchanan for taking the time out of your busy schedule to help mama with this project. I truly appreciate your kindness.

  And a very special thanks to all others behind the scenes that may have assisted in any way with the book coming to life.

Introduction

  This book Infinity contains an infinite amount of written beauty expressed through each of the poems composed by the author. The author Jacqueline James will take you on an amazing journey of humility and peace as she brings to life her authentic poetry.
  You will find harmony as well as pleasure when exploring the creativity expressed within each poem. The poems are designed to inspire, motive, educate as well as entertain you when exploring page after page after page.

Chapter 1
General

1. Fight or Flight...
2. The Golden Seniors...
3. The Move...
4. My Stuff...
5. Don't Run...
6. Pressure Bust Pipes...
7. Sorry...
8. The Plan...
9. Lack of Attention...
10. Not a "Friend"...
11. Be Like U...
12. The Best of my Night...
13. The "new"...
14. Negative Energy...
15. I Have Poems...

Fight or Flight...

For all of us who has a vision, or an appetite for success;
Working hard during the day on through the night
trying to project our best:
Fight or flight-fight for what you believe in,
Digging way drown deep, for your strength within:
You can work long and hard with strong conviction;
Or you can take off in flight and run to make provisions:
Nevertheless it's your decision;
Make it count, with strong convictions:
You can stand up, and fight for what you believe in;
Or take off in-flight, and never ever attempt to win:
Be fully engaged in your decision;
There's no instructions, or supervision:
Everything is done within a blink;
So you must rely on your own instinct:
That's no chance to second-guess;
Just, make a wise choice, then try your best:
If you choose to stand up and fight;
Then fight until the day, loses its light:
If you prefer it's better to take off in flight;
Then run run fast, with all your might.

JACQUELINE JAMES

The Golden Seniors

The golden seniors filled with experiences and knowledge;
Blessed to be given the 'Holy Ghost' power:
We all look up to them, for compliance:
For their support, and also their guidance;
They've work diligently, from day to night;
While viewing the world, through Jesus light:
They're all the role models, that I choose to have;
Who constantly sacrifice, on my behalf:
They never gave up, when their struggles became hard;
They just fast and pray, and turn it over to the Lord:
Blessed be those, who led our path;
For those are footprints, to Jesus hands:
They've faced many obstacles, over the years;
Some of their challenges, may have brought about countless tears:
Nevertheless, they've survived with great wisdom, to share;
They're always willing to help guide our youth, because they care:
Living righteous, throughout their days;
And, never hesitating to give God the praise:
For God has blessed them with His love that lingers;
Let always celebrate, with great honor, our 'Golden Seniors'

INFINITY

The Move...

The move, with a lots "working bees", was expected to go smooth;
But, it was time consuming, all through the morning, until late in the afternoon:
If you think we were done, then you're not right;
We kept right on working until the day lost its light:
It was seven of us working hard,
with each assigned to our own part;
To make the move organized from the start:
I was put on kitchen duty, which was supposed to be simple;
However, I ran out of boxes, which put me in a dilemma:
While my son went out to get more boxes from the store;
I decided to just cleanup, a little more:
Then, he returned, later on in the day;
With newspapers, and more boxes to pack the dishes away:
When I finished with the kitchen, I thought I was through;
But, I looked around, and there was plenty of work to do:
So, I went into the living room to pack up the closet;
It was filled with coats, games, umbrellas, and seasonal blouses:
Then I got a big box, and popped it in place;
And, I filled it to the rim, without any hast:
I looked around for other things to pack;
And, it was pictures on the wall, and plants on a rack:
I went down the hall to check the children room;
It was still junkie, so I needed a broom:

Jacqueline James

The guys were working, loading up the moving truck;
With the couches, and bedroom furniture, and all the heavy stuff:
The truck had to be returned by 2 p.m.
Which put us in a strain, and out on a limb:
My son went to get my pickup truck,
cause we weren't done moving yet;
But, when he got back one of the tires was on a flat:
So, we rode around to find a shop to get the tire fixed;
The tire was fixed by 5p.m., but storage closed at six:
So, we loaded much as we could onto truck;
We made in time to the storage, it was just our luck:
Despite of our efforts we tried our best;
But, it had gotten in too late, to move the rest:
So, the next morning we started again;
But, this time we was minus a friend:
Now it was six of us working, that was left;
And, we worked hard together to pack the rest:
When we finished it was late in the evening;
And, it was neatly stored, you better believe it,
So, we vacuumed, mopped and clean the house;
We, got it neat and livable for the next family to come about.

My Stuff

Someone try to walk away with all of my stuff;
He had my stuff in a bag, too small to carry:
He left with my stuff, and he left in a hurry:
I was tired, and I almost let him get away;
He was far from my reached, at the end of my day:
He rolled it up, then stuffed it into a sack;
Then moved quickly, with it over his back:
He held my confidence, my joy, and my self-esteem;
He walked right past me, with my hopes and dreams:
He grabbed my dignity, and my pride;
Then he balled it up, and stuff it inside:
He took my drive, alone with my motivation;
And, crushed it completely, to satisfy his situation:
He held my vision, in order for me to push forward;
I was in silence, and scared as a coward:
However, he left the spirit, of my existence;
And, my incentive made me persistent:
So, I stopped him before he closed the chapter;
And, wrote me off, as if nothing had happen:
Then, I retrieve all of my creativity;
And, I shaped it into something that I would believe:
First, I took back my joy, for my day;

Jacqueline James

And, I developed something that was sure to stay:
Then I grabbed up all of my self-esteem;
And, I pushed myself, to the extreme:
Next, I took up my stubborn pride;
And, knockout obstacles, so I can survive:
Then, with all of the dignity left in me;
I proved to myself, what I could be:
So, when he walked out of my life, he didn't take much;
He may have taken his things, but he didn't get my stuff.

Don't Run...

Don't run when the road gets rough;
Put on your 'big-pants' and get tough:
Sometimes situations get complicated;
But they can be defeated, when you're dedicated:
You might not have all the right answers;
But you can search for solutions, through every measure:
Whatever don't kill you, will make you stronger;
So, just push forward, to go on for a little longer:
When the road gets rough, and it's no longer fun;
Whatever you do, don't give up and don't you 'run'!

JACQUELINE JAMES

Pressure bust pipes…

Pressure busts pipes;
Too much tension, can cause a fight:
Keep pushing, and pushing, until you lose control;
Enough pressure, can make anyone explode:
A buildup of anxiety, in plain sight;
Can transform into violence, before the day losses it's light:
Build-up, build-up, build-up, now pop!
Unresolved issues, will never stops:
Address your situations, and do it fast;
If you don't, then they're going to crash:
Then you'll end of doing something, that you'll regret;
And, those who witness it, will never forget:
Before you become all anxious, and possibly hyped;
Don't you forget 'pressure' bust pipes!

INFINITY

Sorry...

Sorry for all the things, we didn't do;
Sorry all the things, that hurt you:
Sorry for all the moons, that didn't shine;
Sorry for all the empty glasses of wine:
Sorry for all the 'suns', that that didn't set;
Sorry for all of this, and all of that:
Sorry for all the love, that you missed;
Sorry for all the love, I didn't get:
Sorry for all nights, I didn't stay;
Sorry for all the lost time, in our day:
Sorry for me, and sorry for you;
Sorry for all the things, I put you through:
Sorry for all the dances, you didn't 'spin';
Sorry for all the tomorrows, that didn't begin:
Sorry for the promises, that were made;
Sorry for the 'way', that wasn't paved:
Sorry for all the 'sorrows', that brought you pain;
Sorry for all the 'sorrows', that I'm the blame:
Sorry for all the I love, I didn't give;
Sorry for all the 'sorrows', that you feel:
Sorry for not making a better 'way';
Sorry for all the 'sorrow', I didn't say!

JACQUELINE JAMES

The Plan...

At the meeting nobody there wanted to compromise;
And, things started to get complicated, before my eyes:
Lucky for me, I was able to recognize;
But, it came to them, as a big surprise:
Everyone there wanted things to go their way;
And they became confrontational, before the end of the day:
All of this nonsense, over a business plan;
And, I had the proposal in my hand:
It was so much controversy in the room;
I feared it would become violent, very soon:
So, I laid the plan on the table;
And, I begin discussing the start-up label:
They acted as if they didn't understand;
So, they became delusional, and then they ran:
I heard someone shout "run fast as you can":
And, I know that wasn't part of the plan:
I ran after them, to see what happened;
Then I found out, it was their captain:
They were on assignment from their unit;
And, they aborted their mission, and they all knew it:
They were minutes from being 'AWOL'
When they decided, to neglect it all:
But, they saw their 'commanding officer' in charge;
They imagined the consequences, and became alarmed:

INFINITY

So, none of their actions were really intent;
It was all' just supposed to have been an experiment;
They were trying to provoke a reaction;
So, it was me, they were really testing;
However, when they saw their captain, they ran on-demand;
Which had nothing to do with my business plan.

Lack of Attention...

Extreme neglect and lack of attention;
Creates harmful situations with things, I dare not to mention:
Careless behavior and unruly acts;
Lead to consequences, you will regret:
The more you risk and take a chance;
You're most likely to have bad circumstances:
If you have too much time on your hands;
You might give in to life demands:
If you choose to ignore or neglect;
It might just lead to a munch of rejects:
If you don't take the time to pay attention;
You might fall 'short', to the things I've mentioned:

'Not a friend'...

It doesn't matter how long you've known a person;
What matters is how much, you've gotten to know them:
When you take a person out of their comfort zone;
Then you'll find out, what's really going on:
The people who you think, 'got your back';
Are the very ones, trying to stab you, in your back:
These people will embarrass you, everywhere;
They'll try to get you worked up, and knock you off your 'square':
Unfortunately, you'll find out, that they were never your friend;
They just stayed in your life, and tried to pretend:
These people were jealous of you, from the start;
And, took your kindness for weakness, then broke your heart:
Eventually, their 'lies', had to end;
Then you saw that they were not a friend:

Be Like U...

I've always wanted to be like you!
I just didn't know what to do:
When you were fast I wanted to run;
Let down my hair and have some fun:
When you was slow I wanted to sit;
I almost decided to give up and quit:
When you were happy it made me smile;
And I stayed happy for a while:
When you were sad I wanted to cry;
It upset me terribly I can't deny:
When you were hurting I felt your pain;
When you were down it drove me insane:
When you prayed I wanted to praise;
And, thank 'Our Savior', for my days:
When you were up I wanted to jump;
It gave me strength to get over my 'hump';
When you were compassionate I wanted to care;
When you were given I learned to share:
When you was helpful it taught me to give;
I learnt humility as I lived:
But when you were short I just stood still.

INFINITY

The best of my night...

The best of my night, when my child seen me
for the very first time;
He recognizes the scent-that scent is mine:
And admired his beauty, that I put inside;
The universe paused to bow down for 'them';
Our love was captured-how love was meant;
He welcomed me into his world, unlike never before:
My very presence, enhanced his spirit more:
He unlocked the side of him, that was free and in control;
I was there to witness, the beauty he holds:
That night unlike many, we made a real connection;
Our bond was so complete, it reached perfection:
I was very pleased, oh so very proud;
How he handled himself, amongst the crowd:
I seen his independence, and well-rounded spirit;
I seen his bravery, and his strength-you could hear it:
That moment felted so good, it was the best of my night;
When you see what you put into your child, comes out just right:
What I put in him, and what life brought him;
And, all the things he created for himself, was just right for him:
Just to watch his rhythm and charismatic ways;
Made me want my night, to continue for days:
I understood his overwhelming need for 'self';
And, the respect I felt for him was even stronger, when I left:

JACQUELINE JAMES

The 'New'...

My life is sometimes complicated;
On any day, I don't regret it:
None of my memories, will I forget them;
They're all mine, and I'll just collect them:
If I wrote them down, it would be poor taste;
Because, if I had to relive them I'll hesitate:
I leave them there, were they belong;
And, let my life go right alone:
I moved on to new memories, to start again;
To pick up new thoughts, and make new friends:
Out with the 'old', and in with the 'new';
That's exactly what I'm going to do.

INFINITY

Negative Energy...

There's negative energy surrounding me;
I just want to stay peaceful and sweet:
I don't need animosity, and that's for certain;
Because, I'm a humble, and pleasant person:
I insist that this negativity cease;
So, I that may continue my day in peace:

Ok, someone called you a nasty word;
Now you're upset over what you heard:
If they don't take it back, doesn't mean it's true;
You can't allow what people say,
defined you;
Nor, can you allow what people do or say,
get you bent out of shape;
Then, they'll have control of you, for goodness sake:

I know it's easier said than done;
But, if you allow them to get you all worked up, then that's no fun:
Negative energy can come in through many forms;
Sometimes we're provoked, which may cause harmed:
It can even come from, the ones we love the most;
They can get besides themselves, like other folks:
Regardless, of who invites the negative conversation;
We must remain calm, and peaceful through the situation:
Because once provoked, then it's on you;

JACQUELINE JAMES

And, you will begin to act negative too:
It's a 'domino effect', that's for sure;
Then you'll be responding with thoughts unclear:
Your actions will be all out of character,
from what you normally do;
You'll start to exert negative energy too:
Yes, it's contagious and it spreads quickly like a fire out-of-control;
So, be cautious of the people that you choose to expose:

You want to contain it, as quick as you can;
So, you can go back to being happy, that is the plan:
Next time don't allow your time to become a waste;
Eliminate the people, that brings negative energy to your space:

INFINITY

I Have poems…

I have poems that manifest itself physical;
I have physical attributes, that manifest itself into a poem:
I have poems that manifest itself, into an attribute:
I bear witness that I have seen this, and this is true;
I bear witness that I have seen this, and bear witness to you:
Before now I seen hope in your eyes;
In your eyes, I seen hope, as I stood by your side:
Those things of despair, that was missing from you;
From you despair was missing, and you knew it, to be true:
No regrets to be found, within you;
Within your characters, no regrets were found:
I write of truths from things that emerged;
Emerge where the things, I wrote of their truth:
Poems I have from their meanings;
From their meanings, I have poems.

Chapter 2

Spiritual

1. Only Through Jesus...
2. Only God Knows...
3. Jesus Therapy...
4. Greatness in me...
5. You Let Your "Angel" Slip Away...
6. FEAR-NOT...
7. I'm Healed...
8. Holy Women...
9. Holy Women on One Accord...
10. Holy Women Working for God Promises...
11. Holy Women Standing on the Promises of the Lord

Only Through Jesus...

You won't be humble and you won't stay sane;
Until you call on Jesus name:
Your heart will honor, what your ears have heard;
Once you acknowledge the "Masters", word:
Hold your wrath, and your anger will cease;
Cause, God will keep you, in his perfect peace:
Trust in His love, and keep your faith;
It's only through Jesus, will you find your grace.

Only God Knows...

Only God knows the end plan for me;
After I follow His close instructions, that's when I'll be able to see:
Only God knew the pain that I felt;
The ache that was in my heart from the pain that was real:
Only God knew when I'm in desperate need of relief;
Because of my faith, I was comforted through my belief:
Only God knew when I tried, and my soul was hurt;
It was in His perfect will, and I did not dessert:
Only God knew the trouble I was going through;
He sent his only begotten son, to bring me through:
Only God knew when I was weighed down with burdens;
He only gave me as much as I could bare, and that's for certain:
Only God knows what's best for me;
He gives me blessings, that I have not room enough to receive:

Jesus Therapy…

For all the struggles in life, that I go through, while I'm alive;
I need some Jesus therapy, to help me to survive:
I'm not calling the doctor, to fill me up with some pills;
And, I don't need drugs, or alcohol to give me a cheap thrill:
I know Jesus is a Savior, and His love is for real;
But, it's my prayer, and supplication, that seals the deal:
Whenever I'm feeling down, or in doubt;
It's my faith in Jesus, that's brings me out:
Jesus is my comforter, in my time of need;
And, He's "my way maker", that help me to succeed:
Whenever I'm burden with a heavy load;
I allow Jesus to take full control:
When I'm facing sickness, and my body's weak;
Jesus heals my body, and makes me complete:
If sadness comes, and leave me feeling low;
It's Jesus's word that picks me up, and stay with me as I go,
I'm truly grateful to have Jesus's therapy;
Because of it, I have no worries:

JACQUELINE JAMES

Greatness in me…

I'm awake during the night working hard;
Cause, you bring out the greatness in me, Lord:
You make my night shiny, so I can be bright;
And the world sees my talent, when the day gives its light:
I reflect your greatness, as I achieve;
You fill me with awesome, I do believe:
Your love allows me to express my greatest style;
And, it's one of the reason, why I smile:
You keep me humble, and You keep me meek;
So, my greatness through You, will be complete:
The blessings You give, as I pray;
Fills me with Your greatness, that's here to stay:

INFINITY

You Let Your 'Angel', Slip Away...

God placed an 'angel' before you;
Who admired and adored you:
You dismissed the 'gift', she brought to share:
When you intentionally choose to ignore her:
You allowed your pride to control your day;
And, you let your 'angel' slip away:
Now, she has spread her wings in another direction;
Covered under God's protection:
You never knew you had an 'angel' in your presence;
Perhaps you would've been cautious, before you dismissed your treasure:
She was never a threat to you;
She was only sent, to help see you through:
God wanted you to know that His miracles comes through different forms;
Some of us preach, and some of us are blessed with poems:
God needed you to appreciate the art of His love;
Because, everything that's good comes from above:
God wanted you to receive a blessings from His word;
Which, He sent through her gentle voice to be heard:
But, you allowed your ego to control your day;
And, eventually your 'angel' slipped away:

FEAR-NOT...

F = Faithfulness is believing in things to come to past;
Knowing that God's goodness is going to last:
Stepping out of your comfort zone and trusting in God;
Knowing you're be blessed, cause you're His child:
Proclaiming many miracles in your life;
Speaking it aloud, bringing it into the light:

E = Everlasting love that's just right for me;
Shinning so brightly for the whole world to see:
Holding on to its richness throughout my destiny;
Embracing His glory through all eternity:

A = Angels of the Lord watching over my life;
Helping me silently through my fight:
Keeping me safe while I sleep during the night;
Watching over me closely to the morning light:
Always sheltering me from my storm;
Cradling me safety in His arms:

R = Relentlessly pushing me toward Jesus's light;
Rewarding me when I'm during things that's right:
Recognizing the accomplishments in my life:
Remembering my strength comes from my Savior Jesus Christ:

INFINITY

N = Nurturing all the future generations to come;
Teaching them the greatest that they came from:
Never once fearing the unknown;
Knowing with Christ you're not alone:

O = Opportunity to live holy and blessed;
Without any worries or stress:
Opening up your heart to Jesus Christ;
To be the spiritual leader of your life:

T = Trusting in His Holy name;
He'll never leave you the same:
Praying and praising for God's good grace;
Trusting to see Our Father's face:

I'm Healed...

I'm healed, from the dishonesty you showed toward me;
I'm healed, because I trusted in God to set my soul free:
I'm healed, from all the anger, I felt toward you;
I'm healed, because God took his right hand of power, and brought
me through:
I'm healed, because I let go of the past, in order to forgive;
I'm healed, because God said showing compassion,
is the way I should live:
I'm healed, past your arrogance, and your lies;
I'm healed, after God revealed the truth before my eyes:
I'm healed, past the disappointments, from your betrayal;
I healed, because God delivered me with Christian behavior:
I healed, because I'm blessed through the Lord Jesus my Savior:
I'm healed, because God my Father showed me favor:

Holy Women...

The women of clarity, and of great stature;
Uplifting and inspiring, working hard with virtue:
These are the ladies, that I choose to admire;
The ones that's not filled, with greed, lust, or desire;
They are true women, set-a-side, for the Lord;
Never complaining, when their tasks, becomes hard:
Always willing to give a loving hand;
And, render service to others, on God's command:
Blessed are these women, anointed under God's word;
Set-a-side for the 'Master's use, and chosen to be heard:
Studying, and worshiping under one roof;
Learning God's word, and excepting his 'truths';
Grace be given to these women, in the church;
Who fellowship together, giving God the 'glory' first:
Forever helping, and nurturing, showing kindness above all;
And, always available, when the work from the Lord calls:
God's perfect plan that He has for every woman, equal to a man;
Yet different roles, and that she understands,
Never purposely bringing attention to themselves;
Only expressing God's commandment, and denying the rest:
Above all expressing Jesus love;
These of the 'Holy' women with righteousness comes:
For in their hearts they hide God's words,
And, through their actions His 'spirit' is heard:

JACQUELINE JAMES

Holy Women on One Accord...

Thank you Jesus for giving me the mindset to be on one accord;
Without the power of the 'Holy Ghost', my life will be hard:
Philippians 2:1-8
1 If there be therefore any consolation in Christ, if any comfort of love, if any fellowship of the spirit, if any bowels of mercies;
Put God first in your life, and he will reward you with certainties:
2 Fulfill ye my joy, that ye be like-minded, having the same love, being of one accord, of one mind;
With God's word in your heart then Jesus peace, you shall find:
3 Let nothing be done through strife or vainglory, but in lowliness of mind, Let each esteem other better than themselves;
Building each other up through the body of Christ saving souls is what's left:
4 Look not every man of his own things, but every man also of the things of others;
Because of it God called Joseph to be Jesus father, and Mary to be his mother:
5 Let this mind be in you which was also in Christ Jesus;
Because He sacrifice His life, for that reason:
6 Who being in the form of God, thought it not robbery to be equal to God;
7 But made himself no reputation, and took upon him the form of a

servant, and was made in the likeliness of men;
Allowing us to keep the commandments, and live a life of righteousness, without sin
8 And being found in fashion as a man, he humbled himself and became obedient until death, even the death of the cross;
Us showing submissiveness unto God humbling ourselves, through Jesus blood he paid our cost:
For the Holy women standing on the promises of the Lord;
Staying obedient to His word, and worshiping on one accord:

Jacqueline James

Holy Women Working for God's Promises

It is some stipulations and regulations to receive the promises of
the Lord;
That is to remove thy self from self and release thy 'vanity', and
work hard:
Proverbs 31:30
*Favor [s] deceitful and beauty [is] vain [but] a woman [that]
feareth the Lord shall be praised;*
And, she shall be blessed throughout her days:
Psalms 119:37
*Turn away mine eyes from beholding vanity [and] quicken thou me
in thy way;*
So that I may feel the spirit of the Lord throughout my day:
1st Samuel 16:7
*But the Lord said unto Samuel look not on his contenance or on
the height of his statue; Because I have refused him; For [the
Lord seeth] not as man seeth: for man looketh on the outward
appearance, but the Lord looketh on the heart:*
Faithfulness allows us as 'Holy' women to do our part:
Your hair may be fixed, your nails are done, with your jewelry on,
and your clothing matching all the way down to a 'T';
But God said is your heart, ready to receive me?

INFINITY

Matthew 6:1-7
1 Take heed that ye do not your alms before men, to be seen of them, otherwise you have no reward of your father which is in heaven;
2 therefore when thy doest thine alms do not sound a trumpet before thee, as the hippocrates in do the synagogues, and in the street that they may have glory of men. Verily I say unto you, they have their rewards;
3 But when thy doest thy alms, let not thy right hand know what thy left hand doeth:
4 That thine alms be in secret and the Father that seeth in secret himself shall reward you openly;
5 And when thou prayest thou shall not be as the hypocrites are; for they love to pray it standing in the synagogue and in the corners of the streets that they may be seen of men;
Verily I say unto you they have their rewards:
6 But thou when thou prayest, enter into thy closet and when thou hast shut the door, pray to thy Father which is in secret, and thy Father which seeth in secret shall reward thee openly;
7 But when ye pray do not use vain repetitions as the heathens do; for they think that they should be heard for their many speakings;
8 Be not ye therefore like unto them: for your Father knoweth what things ye have need of, before ye ask him:

Therefore discipline thy self in God's word to be blessed:
God doesn't want a woman to be voluptuous,
for the world to desired;
However, he's looking for a 'Holy' woman that's virtuous, through her works to be admired:

JACQUELINE JAMES

Holy Women Standing on the Promises of the Lord...

Holy women standing on the promises of the Lord;
As a Christian her bond is form;
She a 'Holy' woman, standing on the promises of our Lord:
In 2 Peter 1:4
Whereby are given unto us exceeding great and precious promises;
that by these ye might be partakers of divine nature, having escape
the corruption that is in the world through lust;
Through our faith we are made whole, in God we trust:
With the 'spirit' within us, we cannot fall;
Trusting in Our Lord and Savior as our all:
In the scriptures given by God we find righteousness;
Through which his inspiration for instructions is meant:
In *Jeremiah 29:11*
For I know the thoughts that I think toward you, saith the Lord,
thoughts of peace, not of evil to give you an expected end;
And God sent his only begotten son Jesus to die on 'Calvary' to be
our savior and our friend:
God said
In *Matthew 11:28*
Come unto me all ye that labour and or heavy laden and I will give
you rest;
Because of his promise, we're able live, and be blessed:

INFINITY

In *Matthew 11:29 God said*
Take my yoke upon you and learn of me; for I am meek and lowly in heart and ye shall find rest unto your souls;
Through our submission in God's word, we allow him to take control:
When the 'Holy' women stand on God's promises, they're 'full', which makes them whole;
It enriches their lives, and saves their souls:
In *Isaiah 40:29*
He giveth power to the faint; and to them that have no might he increaseth strength;

There's power in the name Jesus, in which God sent:
Isaiah 40:30-31
30 even the youths shall faint and be weary and the young men shall utterly fall 31 But they that wait upon the LORD shall renew their strength, they shall mount up, and not be weary, and they shall walk, and not faint;
These are the 'Holy' women of the Lord standing on God's promises, worthy to be named His Saints:
In *Philippians 4:19*
And my God shall supply all your needs according to his riches in Glory by Christ Jesus;
And, Jesus was our sacrificial lamb for that reason:
In *Romans 8 37-39*
Nay in all these things we are more than conquerors through him that loved us 38 for I am persuaded that neither death, nor life, nor angels, nor principalities, nor powers, nor things present, nor things, to come 39 nor height, nor depth, nor any creature shall be able to separate us from the love of God which is Christ Jesus our Lord;
Because of God's promises boldly may I speak, with Him in charge:
Jesus said
In *John 14:27*
Peace I leave with you, my peace I give unto you; not as the world giveth, give I unto you. Let not your heart be troubled, neither let It

be afraid:
That is God's purpose of our creation, that is the reason we were made:
Through their thirst for righteousness as they seek;
Their 'Holiness' keeps them humble, and keeps them meek:
They are disciplined by God's word with strong convictions;
And, Jesus blood is their protection:
Life situations may test their faith, when times get hard;
However, they are the 'Holy' women standing on the promises of the Lord:

INFINITY

Chapter 3
Educational
1. The President...
2. The Winners...
3. Being...Doesn't...
4. Provoked...
5. Police Brutality...
6. Them 2 Days...
7. U Can't Buy Loyalty...
8. 1 Million-to-Infinity...

The President...

Now he's well into his presidency;
And the majority of the public wants him impeached:
Doing all his campaign strategies, he tried to be slick;
Now, he's showing all of his deep-rooted prejudice:
This man's not a leader, he's a racist;
And, what makes him think, that the country's okay with it?
He allowing the 'KKK', to discriminate;
And, kill 'Blacks' & 'Hispanics' , from state-to-to:
He wants to start a civic war;
Where civilians will be walking down the streets, always armed:
He's trying to start a World War;
Without any 'allies' to even the score:
But, it's innocent lives he'll be taken;
To boost his ego, and his ratings:
This man is demonic, with a death-wish;
He won't step down, so we need to insist;
Congress needs to release the records, of his mental state;
Cause, this man is very evil, and he's full of hate:
He's unstable and he's very insecure;
However, he's our president, so we must endure:
He has no regard for the human life;
And, these foreign affairs, are not our fight:
I don't know how much longer society can handle this;
Because, his human instinct, cease to exist:

All of his personal friends have left his side;
Because, they refuse to tolerate, his 'evil' inside:
He never had any ones best interest in mind;
And, now that he's the 'president', he doesn't try to hide:
He fired the 'staff' that might have done our country some good;
So, that his corruption would dominate, if it could:
We need to take actions, to turn this situation around;
Before his oblivious 'plot' reach solid-ground:
Any solutions?, because I'm open for suggestions;
This "president's" leadership is up for questioning

The Winners...

Taught to compete, bred to be the best;
From the preschool games, to the grade school spelling test:
Always practicing for something bigger than themselves;
With hard work, and perseverance never accepting anything less:
Being discipline to stay focused, with complete concentration;
Always motivated, to show total dedication:
Constantly entering all sorts of competitions;
To test their skills, and develop their performance:
Living a life driven, only by their passion;
Continuously pushing, for complete satisfaction:
Trapped in an illusion, that everything should be right;
Never sleeping from the day, to the night:
Sacrificing all, without any exceptions;
Dreaming a dream, that's filled with deception:
Stressing unlike any level of comprehensive;
Defeating all odds, to become the 'winners':
Determining to reach the level of perfection;
Never backing down, under any circumstances:
Proving to the world, that they're better than most;
Because they're 'winners', unlike other folks:

Being... Doesn't...

Being handicap, doesn't mean you're disabled;
Being disable, doesn't make you handicapped:
Depression can make you sad;
But, sadness doesn't have to make you depressed:
Being without, doesn't make you weak;
Being weak, doesn't make you without:
Being lonely, doesn't mean you're alone;
Being alone, don't make you lonely:
Being rich, doesn't make you happy;
Being happy, doesn't mean you're rich:
Being natural, doesn't make you real;
Being real, don't mean you're natural:
Being controlling, doesn't mean you're in control;
Being in control, don't make you controlling:
Telling the truth, does make you truthful;
Telling a lie, does make you a liar!

Provoked...

Provoked to get my hands dirty;
And, my feet wet in the sand:
For the rights of all, equally I stand:
Just to know, it doesn't existence deeply angers me;
I can only imagine the distraught from the ones,
who've actually seen:
Being gunned down in broad daylight, in the middle of the road;
And, being dismissed as waste, as if you're trash or something old:
While your loved ones witness this horrific event;
All this injustice brought on by the 'ones'
who sworn to serve and protect:
They're the police killing our 'people' mercilessly;
Leave our homes with pain, and emptiness:
Who's going to cry for our sons, and daughters,
as they lie in the street to die?
While their blood shed across the pavement, and their 'souls'
float in the sky:
So we form a 'rally', and we protest marching on;
We've all come together, and through our faith
we're standing strong:
What about the next generation of our children
that comes through?
Should we tell them at 'birth', because they're 'black' they might
be gunned-down too?

Jacqueline James

Now I've become agitated, I'm all worked up;
Because, of this senseless killing, I'm stricken with disgust:
So, I speak out and my word spread like a wildfire;
Vengeance with vigilante justice, is what I truly desire:
I was once calm, and peaceful as can be;
However, you provoked me,
raging up a spirit of 'hatred' inside of me:
I demand justice for all of my people's blood;
These are the lives of our 'babies' that 'you' continue
to sweep, under-the-rug:
I'm asking you to help me satisfy this 'itch' that
needs to be 'scratched':
By (terminating) the police officers, and not allowing them,
to come back:
When my answers go unsatisfied leaving me without hope;
I'm force to result to desperate measures,
because I've been 'provoked'!.

Police Brutality...

The police are killing "black" people as well as "gays";
And, the government has allowed their actions to continue, over months and days
There's no reason for their brutality;
Hatred and prejudice is what motivates, this reality:
They've taken several lives, without a doubt;
This senseless killing, just has to STOP:
They're also targeting "gays", "transgenders", "bisexuals", and "lesbians";
Because, of their differences, they're trying to eliminate them:
Black and white activists have come together for peaceful protests;
To stand up for "Black lives", "LGBTQ", and the rest:
However, there's nothing's peaceful when it comes to the police;
They're invoking violence, using 'mace', 'Billy-clubs', and 'tasers', to say the least:
They're in direct violation of their authority;
But, their actions are never subjected to any consequences regardless:
I'm looking for answers, but I'm not searching on my own;
I may be one voice speaking, but I'm not alone:
They could be hurting your son, daughter, or someone you love, they're never going to stop;
Without, any consequences for the actions-they're just not!
Families are left heartbroken, scared in an outrage While, hopelessness, and despair fills their days:

It's time to pull together, and react from their actions;
The malice is coming from the police who vow
to serve, and give us protection:
We can't put our trust in this 'uniform' man;
We must pull together as a whole in- order-to make a stand:
Let's make this message go viral so that the nation will hear us;
We must do more than just talk, we must keep up a 'fuss':

Them 2 days...

You can reschedule any days of the year;
But you can't change your birthday;
And, you can't change your death day;
Them 2 days, that sets you apart:
What you do in between, those two days;
Is your adventures in life-it's your personal maze:
At birth you can't control it, but it's recorded;
Growing up, you make your own destiny
which is sometimes rewarded,:
We go through life trying to find, that peace from within;
And, the older we get, the harder we fight, cause we know it's
getting closer to our end:
Sometimes we leave here, without any notice, or any warning;
Other times, were given a 'death sentence',
and we know it's soon coming:
Either way it's recorded, that rememberable day;
And, regardless of 'it's' reason, God did it His way:
You can count your days, that you're here on this 'Earth';
However, you can't reschedule, your 'death' or your 'birth':

U can't buy loyalty…

Loyalty you can't buy it, it's not for sale;
When a person is loyal, then you can tell:
When you're looking for 'truth', it don't need no support;
The loyalty you'll find, will come from the heart:
You'll know when someone is a 'stand-up', person;
Because, they'll be there for you, and that's for certain:
They'll render their services, no matter what;
And, go the distance, without any fuss:
Regardless of the cost, they won't turn their back;
Because, true loyalty, will pick up the slack:
They can't be bribed, with a price;
Because of their loyalty they'll sacrifice:
And, they'll never complain, about the things they've lost;
Because, true loyalty, just can't be bought:

INFINITY

1 Million -To- Infinity

It's 1 million to Infinity different things to do;
Try them all, one will be just right for you:
Be selective when you go about your day;
Make your time count, do things your way:
If the first thing you choose doesn't work, then try something else;
Whatever you do, give it your best:
Don't use substitute, or settle for less;
Keep moving forward, to pass life's test:
Don't you dare look back on yester-years;
It's a waste of time, and a waste of tears:
Try something new, and if by chance you fall;
Pick up your pieces, and humbly stand tall:
It's a million to infinity different things to do;
Find the one that's just right for you:

Jacqueline James

INFINITY

VV

Chapter 4

Informative

1. Don't Forget 2 Love You 4 You...
2. Surviving the "Storm"...
3. Taxes...
4. I Love all my Imperfections...
5. The "Victims"...
6. What is a Friend...
7. I Trusted...
8. High Self-esteem...
9. My Girls...
10. Where will my soul go...
11. The After Mask...

INFINITY

Don't Forget 2 Love You 4 You....

When mama forget to love you,
And daddy forget to love you,
When your sisters forget to love you,
And your brothers forget to love you,
Don't you forget to love you,
Be the most important person to you,
When the your friends forget to love you,
And your cousins forget to love you,
The neighbors forget to love you,
And the community simple forgets,
Give yourself all the love, and hugs you can possibly get,
When your dog forget to love you,
Or your cat forget to love you,
Your boss forget to love you,
And, your coworkers forget to love you,
What's the matter?, you haven't loved on you yet?
Loving on you, is what you need to do,
When your spouse forget to love you,
And your children forget to love you,
All your aunt's forgot love you,
Your uncle's forgot to love you,

JACQUELINE JAMES

Don't You dare forget to love you,
Make sure you care enough to love you,
When the whole world forgets to love you,
Remember God will always love you!
He loves you so much, He sent His only begotten son Jesus to
never forget to love you!
So you need to love you too!

INFINITY

Surviving the "Storm"

Bringing every nationality together,
After several natural disasters,
Scavenging and struggling, making human connections,
Showing humility and affection,
Hurricanes and storms do not discriminate,
You can't fight against them, you must evacuate,
There's no such thing as prejudice when we need to survive,
We all pull together, setting aside our differences
in-order-to stay alive,
From all different walks of life,
We're united for a single fight,
The catastrophic events, that took place 'here',
Knocked each and every one of us, off our 'square',
We were all forced live in ruins,
With 'rations' given, to each one of us,
None of us richer-none of us poor;
Each and every one of us, were camped out on the floor,
Bunched up in shelters, waiting for relief,
At the mercy of others, to feel our grief,
This horrific event to bring families together,
Simply because, we all was affected by bad weather,
We disregarded all nationality, race, and religion,
And, we bond together to form an allegiance,
Surviving the storm it's just the beginning,
The rebuilding and cleanup, is our happy ending.

Jacqueline James

Taxes...

It's honor for me to pay my taxes;
Because, I know I've received more than rations:
I've had a wonderful run in life indeed;
I was given plenty to meet my needs:
I never lived an extravagant life;
I am the mother of five, and I was also a wife:
We accepted the things, that were entitled to us;
And, those that weren't, we didn't make a fuss:
A raised my children to be humble, and meek;
To have strong 'Christian' values, but not to be weak:
We've worked hard to accomplish the things we have;
And, earned the right to relax, and laugh:
All of my children are young adults, as of now;
And, they do the best, that life allows:
Taxes are put in place, to help the ones in need;
If you refuse to pay them, then that's pure greed:
I was once in need, on the receiving end;
Because of it, I'm appreciative my friend:
Some people depend on what others give;
And, taxes are put in place for them to live:
Some people salary comes from our taxes;
And, state wide jobs to make our lives better:
There's school taxes put in place;
To insure education, through every race:

INFINITY

The emergency response teams are paid for through our taxes;
To make sure we get health-care, and also protection:
There's parks paid for, community centers, and roads as well;
So, be responsible and pay your taxes, or simply go to jail:

JACQUELINE JAMES

I Love all my Imperfections...

I love all my imperfections;
Me and myself have made our own connections;
I love me, I love everything about me;
I love everything about me, all the way down to my ingrown hair,
that ain't supposed to be there;
I love the brown and black hair, to all the grey in my head;
To my overgrown toenails, that gets stuck in my bed:
I love my beautiful brown skin, that covers my body;
I love all my freckles, and scars unlike anybody:
I love my wrinkles, scratch marks, and all of my age spots:
I love my 50 extra pounds, and my matted hair-forming locks:
I love the arthritis in my knees, and my brittle old bones;
And, I love the way I enjoy my company,
when I'm left home alone:
I love the way I forget things, then I remember them days later;
And, I love the way I convinced myself, that things
are getting greater:
I love my blood that flows through my veins;
And, I love all my good thoughts, that keeps me sane:
I love my big round belly, to my fat feet;
And, my little pug nose, to my chubby cheeks:
I love my buck-out eyes, to my weak knees;
I love the hair tickling my nostrils, that makes me sneeze:
I love my preciseness, to want everything in it's place;

INFINITY

And, I love when I'm content, with a smile on my face:
I love the three piercing in my ears, to my butterfly tattoo;
And, I love the wounds on my arms,
from the things I went through:
I love my flat chest, to my wide shoulders;
And, I love the way I'm gracefully getting older:
I love all the puzzles in my thoughts;
And, my devotion to figure each one of them out:
I love the gentleness in my tone, as I speak;
And, I love the humbleness I show to the people I meet:
I love the subtleness I have, to hold back my tears;
And, I love the wisdom I've acquired over the years:
I love the way I'm up all night, working with strong convictions;
And, I love the way my back throbs with pain,
that I dare to mention:
I love the way that I gasp, and wheeze sometimes
to catch my breath;
And, I love the way my lungs open wide, to allow the oxygen to
pass through my chest:
I love the way my hair falls slightly, covering my eyes;
And, I love the way my eyes open widely, when I'm scared, or
surprised:
I love the way I can find humor in just about everything,
I do, or say;
And, I love the way I lift my arms up to praise, and the way I kneel
down to pray:
I love all the beauty, that my eyes have seen in my lifetime;
And, I love the way that I compose it all together,
and make it rhyme:
I love the unique styles I wear, when I'm so elegantly dressed;
And, I love showing the world that I'm at peace,
and I am also blessed:
I love when I'm sitting on my front porch so calmly, and content;
And, I love the way I'm mesmerized by the precious thoughts God
sent:
I love the way my flaky skin itches from eczema all day;
And, I love the way I'm soothe from the brightness, of the sun's

ray:
I love the way I get hyper, and sometimes drive myself crazy;
And, I love the way that I'm helpful, and never slouched or lazy:
I love the way I cook so divine, fit for a 'King';
And, I love the way I patiently awaits to be
served as a royal 'Queen':
I love my thunder thighs, and my cellulite;
And, I love the way I stay up working throughout the night:
I love the way I wobble when I walk;
And, I love the way I sometimes stutter, when I talk:
I love the way I laugh out loud, when I'm excited,
and I cry when I'm sad;
And, I love the way I shut down completely,
when you make me mad:
I love my motherhood, and my commitment to my family;
And, I love my mother for taking the time-out to have me:
I love the way I write, and can't remember a word I said;
And I love my 'gift', that you just read:
I love the way I give all the glory to my 'Father' up above;
And, I love the way I show 'His' people, lots of kindness, and love:
I love all of my imperfections and the things I may, or may not do;
Now, can you say, the same thing about you?

The Victims

Unfortunately several people have been tortured, used,
abused, and dehumanized,
These demise have even resorted into untimely deaths, and have
taken authority years to identify,
Sometimes these victims had to identify with their abusers in order
to stay alive,
It was the only defense they had to survive,
They often convinced themselves that the abuse was okay;
Even though they were brought forceful to hideous situations
sometimes they decided to stay,
Any small amount of affection from their abuser made them feel
human again,
And, they start to make a connection, as if they were friends,
It doesn't mean that they accepted what was
done to them or it was okay,
It just meant they were trying to cope, until they got the
opportunity to get away
A lot of them may have endured severe physical scars,
Which may heal, but the damage left behind will be hard,
After being kidnapped, abducted, or (and) held as someone's
personal slave,
All of the surviving victims, may have psychological scars damage
throughout their days,
Some have shut down completely because they couldn't cope,
And, they had to be hospitalized without any hope,

Some of them have turned to alcohol, and drugs, in-order-to deal with their pain,
While others have turn to Jesus, to keep from going insane,
A small percentage of them have taken back their power and said "no more",
And even became vigilantes to settle the score,
However, that's only being a few and a few in between,
A lot of these perpetrators have gotten away with it, and are hiding behind the scenes,
The law should be set in place to better protect human rights,
So the victims don't always have to continue to fight,

I say to all victims who's out there still struggling to survive,
"After such a traumatic ordeal I thank God that He spared your life"

INFINITY

What is a Friend...

Please identify yourself as a friend,
Stop the pretending just to fit in,
Leave your fakeness at the door,
Especially if you choose not deal with me, any more,
My friends are 'here' for me, no matter what,
We get down and dirty if that's what's up,
They'll help in any and every way they can,
Even when it's not particularly in their plans,
We don't have problems speaking what's on our mind,
Because a good friend is hard to find,
Loyalty from me is all you'll get,
I'm the type of friend that's hard to forget,
I'll always give more than I take,
And because of it I've made mistakes,
You can call on me for anything,
And countless 'blessing', with me I'll always bring,
A friend is someone who's caring and kind,
They're understanding, forgiving, and also wise,
Each friend comes with their own unique ways,
To bring a varieties to each other's days,
I'll always appreciate the times that we spend,
Which doesn't have to be every day, to be called a friend,

Jacqueline James

My friends are helpful, loyal, and considerate,
They're genuine, compassionate, and not full of 'it',
A real friend's loyalty, will surpass the rest,
And, if you get just 'one', in a life time, then you're truly blessed.

I Trusted...

I was looking up to someone who meant me no good,
He was 7 years older, and I trusted him like he knew I would,
The things he did to me where discussing and file,
I had to isolate myself to recover for a while,
He used me in so many unspeakable ways,
Which 'zapped' the majority of viable youthful days,
If I'd refuse to do things or even rebel,
He'd slap me around then choke me if I'd yelled,
When I look back I get a horrible image,
How he made me call him 'daddy', and did things I can't mention,
He often told me that he was doing me a favor,
By training me to please any man by my labor,
I wondered why he had me to perform his ungodly needs,
But stricken with shame I never spoke of the deeds,
I trusted him and wanted so much for him to be satisfied,
So I when through the relationship living a lie,
I would put on a 'happy-face' when people saw us together,
I never drop a clue, that he was that type of fellow,
I trusted him when he said that I was the only woman for him, I just needed to be mold,
But later I realized that he was destroying my soul,
He said all the things we did were a secret,
And, that I shouldn't never discuss them with any of my people,

So year after year I kept the secrets inside,
But way down deep they were eating me alive,
When I got older and mature, I broke free from his hold,
Then he became more violent because he lost his control,

But this time I fought back with courage from within,
Because I no longer trusted him, and knew he wasn't my friend,
Now that I'm free, and able to express my voice,
I can find a decent man to date of my own choice.

High Self-esteem...

I may have a few extra pounds but I don't have low self-esteem,
I'm not stuck-up, nor am I mean,
I do not have low self-esteem:
So I refuse accept everything you bring,
If you can't come correct and bring the ring;
Just keep it moving then cause you're not getting a thing,
I'm very wise with common sense,
I refuse to settle for any ones nonsense,
I'm on point with whatever I decide to do,
And, it doesn't include taking 'bull' from you,
Please, I hope that you take this personal,
My time is irreplaceable and my words is irreversible,
I want someone respectful and I'm not settling for nothing less,
Because I'm full of confidence, and I am the best,
So, if you looking for someone who's beneath you, then you're
looking the wrong way,
Because I wouldn't have you, riding, or walking on any given day,
My self-esteem is high so is my expectations,
I refuse to get involved just for relations,
So, please keep it moving, because you're not worth
my conversation,
To my standards I'm fully committed with complete dedication.

Jacqueline James

My Girls...

I came around to get my girls,
In hope that I could, change their world,
To show them all something new,
And leave them fun memories when I'm through,
To make their day a little brighter,
And keep their loads a little lighter,
I hope they see the best in me,
Cause that's exactly what I intend to be,
So they'll see my special side,
I know that they'll enjoy what they find,
I want to change the way they view the world,
Because they are my precious girls.

INFINITY

Where will my soul go…?

When I die, where will my soul go?
Will 'it' float where I won't know?
Will it join my 'late' husband in the sky?
Or will it meet up with my ex-husband, you just died?
I was not my first husband's,- first wife,
But, I was with him, when God took his life,
I was my ex-husband's first wife,
However, we were no longer married, at the end of his life,
So, will my soul just float around,
In search of some sort of stable ground,
Since, I am without a soul mate,
Must I stand single at God's gate?
Or will my soul be split in half,
Because, both 'men' were my better 'half',
While I'm living God fills my void,
Making sure that my life's not hard,
But where will my soul go in my afterlife?
Since I'm no longer a man's wife,
Now that they're no longer here on earth to live,
Am I not the one to complete their ribs?

The After Mask...

Once it started it was ripple effect,
Everyone was fighting over the things that was left,
It's unfortunate when someone dies without a 'will',
And didn't leave instructions for the people that lives,
The ones that's close to 'them', and meant the most,
Those are the ones quelling, not other folks,
Before they even get the person buried into the ground,
They're going through their personal belongings
passing them around,
Some want to 'sell', others want to donate,
Some want to keep everything for themselves and
will do whatever it takes
Sometimes they're not on their best behavior,
So, the courts have to step in to do the labor,
Then there's a 'fee' from the lawyers to the judge,
And, they're left with less to divide and hold a grudge,
This causes the family split up and divided,
And when they're in public, they don't try to hide it,
Burying your love one is a hard enough task,
But it can become overbearing dealing with the after mask.

INFINITY

Chapter 5

Entertainment

1. I Had a Wang-Bang Weekend...
2. My Son Won't Stop Eating...
3. The Television-set...
4. Nacho cheese (Not-your-cheese)
5. Like "scramble-eggs"...
6. See "What had happened was"!
7. This Phone...
8. I Sailed the Sea...
9. Water "mass"...
10. The "70's Party...
11. My House Guest...
12. Under the Shade Tree...
13. Falling Snow...

INFINITY

I Had a Wang Bang Weekend...

I had a wang bang weekend if anyone needs to know,
I had raccoons in my attic and my kitchen ceiling hit the floor,
The maintenance man who came to fix it fell right through,
I looked up and saw him but I had no clue on what to do,

It was Friday evening when all the action started,
I had to deal with the disaster so couldn't go out to party,
When I let my dog out in the middle of the night,
Him and the raccoon had a vicious fight,
They tussle back and forth for at least ten minutes,
My dog grabbed her by the throat and bit right into it,
My dog won the battle, the raccoon laid in my yard dead,
I asked my son to clean it up, but he just shook his head,

I paid a guy to scoop it up with a rack and shovel,
And, he waited until daylight and that was sort of clever,

Then, Saturday afternoon at a quarter after 4,
My son slammed his hand, in my truck door,
So, we spend Saturday evening in the emergency room,
Until the doctor wiped clean, and stitched up his wound,

Jacqueline James

Sunday morning I skipped church for a radio interview,
To discuss my new book that was being released soon,
Afterwards my son "whine" about his finger from being hurt,
So, we met my mother at the store, to buy him some desert,
My daughter came alone to do her grocery shopping,
She filled up a cart and she wasn't stopping,
She wanted me to ride with her to a different grocery store,
First I dropped my son off at home cause he had gotten bored,

My daughter filled her backseat up with groceries and headed to her house,
We had to carry them up 3 flights of stairs but
I didn't open my mouth,
My daughter put up the groceries while I clean up her kitchen,
And, she didn't take me home, until I finish washing her dishes,

When I finally made it home tired and all,
I climbed into my bed and I slept like a log.
So, I had a wang bang weekend if anyone needs to know,
I wouldn't want to relive it and that's for sho!

INFINITY

My son won't stop eating...

My son sits in one spot and eat all the food that he can,
Then tells me "mama you know I'm a growing man",
He 'pigs-out' no doubt, no questions asked,
He eats up all the food, then he eats all the snacks,
At the end of the day I go in my room, and don't come out for a while,
Because, I be tired, and that's just my style,
I don't go to sleep I just don't want to be bothered,
If you need something important, then you need to holla,
I know I leave him in the kitchen unattended,
But I thought we said he was going to eat up everything; he was just pretending,
When I walk through the house, in the middle of the night,
He had eaten all the food, and then turned off the light,
He ate the eggs, he ate the steak, he ate the chicken, and he ate the fish,
He ate the ham, with the cheese and he tried to eat the dish,
He ate the doughnuts, he ate candy, and the gum,
He ate the crackers, and the chips, and didn't leave none,
So, I said to myself I guess in the morning,
I'll go to the grocery store,
Because, when he wakes up, he's going to need to eat some more,
So, I went to the store to buy some fresh stock,
When I came back, he was eating the can-goods,
and just wouldn't stop,

JACQUELINE JAMES

I thought to myself, this man's going to 'pop',
Then I left again to go and buy a lock,
But I must've taken to long,
Cause, when I got back home, all the food was gone,

I said " Man, I'm done; I can't take this no more"!
Then I went to my room and slammed the door!

INFINITY

The television-set...

I was watching the television, until the television start watching me,
There was nothing else showing that I wanted to see,
I turned the power off five minutes later the screen turned bright and then it went blank,
I tried to dismiss what I saw because it had gotten late,
I wasn't tripping something else was controlling my set,
But I wasn't quite ready to analyze it yet,
My head started to hurt as if some sort of 'rays' went through my brain,
Whatever just happened was about to drive me insane,
Once I thought about it I set up for a while,
I said to myself whatever just happened it was pretty-mild,
Something told me to turn on the television set,
Because 'whatever' it was just a bunch of crap,
I didn't know what to watch so I started to channel surf,
I thought I'll settle for whatever news come first,
I was still anxious to know what I just saw,
The news reporters were the ones that covered it alL,
So, I watch the world news for about an hour or so,
But they didn't broadcast anything about a 'light-ray' coming through a blank screen-slow,
Was I just tripping?, I started to second guess myself,
Then I turned off the television and got me some rest.

Nacho cheese...
(Not-your-cheese)...

I made some nachos today but I bought the wrong type of cheese,
I had to scoop hard it didn't come out with ease,
It was clump and thick with a rubbish texture,
I'd never seen cheese in that condition,
I put it in the microwave to try to melt it,
I had to add water first to try to help it,
I only warned it for a minute before it starts sticking to the bowl,
And when I took it out the microwave it was looking old,
I had the tortilla chips, the ground beef, the lettuce, the tomatoes,
and the onions all in their place,
Waiting to top it with cheese I had save some space,
I smooth the lumps out of the cheese with the back of a spoon,
Hoping my family will be hungry enough to eat it up soon,
Some of us use jalapenos others topped ours with sour cream,
But when we taste that cheese we all started to scream!
It was horrible with a capital 'Nasty',
Then one by one the dinner started to get trashy,
No one ate it and I didn't expect them to,
We all threw it away it was the right thing to do.

INFINITY

Like 'scrambled-eggs'...

You must read between the lines,
It's like 'scrambled-eggs' to know what's on my mind,
My thoughts are racing 100 miles an hour,
Like a quiet storm or the steam from a shower,
They're all over the place I can't think of a 'single-thing',
at the same time,
You'll be lucky to climb a mountain to read my mind,
I'll concentrate and stay focused if I could,
Please 'unscramble-the-eggs', if you would!
When you blink your eye I'll change my thoughts,
Now can you tell me what that about?
I'm not confused I'm well aware,
I just can't control all of thoughts that's 'there',
The best I can do is unscramble a few,
In-order-to communicate for a while with you,
The ocean roared and the sea gave way,
Because I decided to talk to you today,
So whatever you get from these few words,
I hope you know they were well deserved,
To get the rest of my thoughts you may have to beg,
Because they're all tangled up, 'like scrambled-eggs'.

JACQUELINE JAMES

See What had Happen was!!!

See what had happen was!!!
The reason why I didn't come over that day to see you;
I had got a flat tire and didn't have a spare so I didn't know what to do,
Well I called the tow services but my membership had expired,
Cause I had to use that money to put some gas in my car to get to work so I wouldn't get fired,
When I had got paid my electric bill was due,
And you know back child support is coming out of my check too,

See what had happen was!!!
I would've called you that night when it had happen but my phone was dead,
And by the time I had got home to charge my phone it was late and I knew you was in the bed,
So I just fixed me something to eat but it had made me sick, and gave me the 'runs'!
And I was up all night with a stomach ache and you know that wasn't fun!
That next morning I had to find me a ride to work,
And you know I can't be talking on the phone at the job cause my boss is a 'jerk'!

INFINITY

See what had happen was!!!
They worked us so hard and didn't none of us got a break;
And when I got off work I had to find a ride to go buy a tire before
it got too late,
By the time I got home I was so tried I went straight to sleep,
And when I woke up the next morning I was feeling weak,
But I managed to go on to work cause you know
I needed that money,

And when I got off that evening, I was worn out I wasn't trying to
call nobody 'honey'!

See what had happen was!!!
That used tire that I had bought it had a slow leak,
And I had been catching the bus to work for the last two weeks,
I didn't call you cause my phone been off I had to use that money
to buy me a 'New' tire,
You know I had to get back and forth to work, I wasn't trying to
get fired,

See what had happen was!
When you was trying to call me you were dialing wrong,
I had to get a new number cause my phone had been
off for too long,
I just scraped up enough money to pay my phone bill,
So you need to be cool and sit down somewhere and chill,

See what had happen was!!!
My new neighbors paid me for helping them move in,
And, the rest I had to borrow from a friend,
You was the first person I called when I got my phone turned on,
Cause I know you've been missing me and holding 'stuff' down on
your own,
Baby you know I miss you too, I'm gonna swing by there to see
you later on tonight,
But when I get there you gonna have to let me hold $20, and on
Friday when I get paid, you know-I'll get you right!

JACQUELINE JAMES

This phone...

I don't think I'm going to like this phone,
I'm trying to text but it's taking too long,
It's not something that I'm used to,
However, I'm going to try my best to make it do-what-it-do,
Is taking me some time to figure it out,
So, I know exactly what the 'apps' are about,
Is hard to type everything down,
When I can't even get the cursor to come around,
I don't know if the screen is cracked,
Or phone itself is just out of whack,
Either way is very slow,
I just thought you might want to know.

INFINITY

I Sailed the Sea...

They prepared a ship, that was appropriate for me,
And, when they were done I'll sailed the sea,
With four canvas 'sail', strong enough to hold,
And, twelve masts of ivory trimmed with gold,
On the side of the ship was an anchor so strong,
Just in case I decided not to sail for long,
And up on the deck waiting for me,
Was a captain seat to make it complete,
The tides, and waves, were all I could see,
As I sailed on and on, my soul was free!

JACQUELINE JAMES

Water 'Mass'...

After the rain a puddle to splash,
Just keep it wet for the fun to last,
A pond to collect the pebbles around,
From every size and shape that hits the ground,
A lake to fish the 'catch' of the day,
A mother to season it and cook it her way,
A stream to float as the wind blows high,
And cast a rainbow in the sky,
A river to paddle on a row boat,
If you stop it still will float,
A waterfall to watch going down the stream,
Beautiful 'waterfall', that holds your dreams,
A beach to swim with sand to play,
To build a castle in midday,
A sea to sail the wonders of the world,
Discovering the mysteries of every boy and girl,
An ocean to dive beneath its core,
To find countless treasures for one to adore.

INFINITY

That '70's Party...

I went to a '70's party from way-back-when,
We had to dress up in 'funky' clothes just to get in,
The men wore bell-bottoms, dashikis, and beanie hats,
Some wore big-wide 'brims', platform shoes,
and stripes, and plaid,
The women wore go-go boots, with mini dresses,
and danced a 'jig',
Other women wore maxi dresses, and big puffy afro wigs,
We all parted-like a 'Cinderella' story,
In spite of our bills regardless of our problems we had no worries,
We just parted,
We danced through the day, and we danced through the night,
We rock and roll to the disco light,
We did the 'bump' and the 'Funky-Chicken',
We made a 'soul-train' line, and the girls walked down switching,
The music played as loud as it could go,
We danced all night, with our big 'afros',
We did the 'Bop', and we even 'slow-danced',
We spin around in our bell bottoms pants,
Some family performed while other's put on a 'skits',
One man spin around and did a 'James Brown' split,
We danced and sang and we ate real good,
We all came out to party and it was 'understood',
We talked and laughed and had a good time,
It was a 'birthday party', but it wasn't mine,

Jacqueline James

I walked around taking lots of pictures,
Because it were good memories and I didn't want to forget them,
I was feeling real good when I left the place,
And I went to sleep that night with a smile on my face.

INFINITY

My House Guest...

My grandchildren came to stay with me for a while,
I had to get used to the teenager's style,
My granddaughter's fourteen,
She walks around all day modeling like a beauty queen,
You will have to be part of the paparazzi's if you want to hang with her,
Because she wants her picture taken all day just for fun,
Let's not talk about her attitude,
It's embedded in her DNA, she's not being rude,
So, if her odd behavior appear to be strange,
She has mood swings when her hormones change,
However, she really is an ordinary girl,
Facebook and Instagram are her entire world,
Now, her brother that came along is an entirely different story,
He's 15 years old and extraordinary,
He loves his video game,
Competing on the internet trying to make yourself a name,
He eats like a racehorse out of energy,
So, I keep my refrigerator stocked with food and plenty,
He's very kind I called him a gentle giant,
He's 6ft 2in, and steady climbing,
He's very helpful around the house,
And if you buy him a new video game, he won't open his mouth,
Now, they came with their two dogs and this is where the challenge began,

JACQUELINE JAMES

I already had a spoil house dog; however,
the dogs never became friends,
They kept their dogs in the basement locked away in a kennel,
But my dog smells their scent, and was constantly trying
to find them,
We let the dogs out in shifts to relieve themselves in the backyard,
But, when it was my dog turn, he sniffs for hours, and to get him
back in-was hard,
My daughter, their mother came as well,
But she works long hours, so you couldn't hardly tell,
When she gets off work, she eats her dinner then lays down,
She doesn't want to be bothered, cause her kids are loud,
But we all had fun together on the weekend,
Because, there's no work, and school is out, so we all stayed in,
It was cool to have them here as my house guest,
I truly enjoyed having them around, because they're the best.

INFINITY

Under the Shade Tree...

Sitting under the big shade tree,
Watching the sun shining down on me,
With no dust discrimination,
I'm one of many kids from the city without recreation,
Something to do on my free time,
Counting the cars as they pass by,
Naming all the ones I wish were mine,
Just innocent fun to pass the time,
Sitting there peaceful as the day is long,
Wanted desperately not to be on my own,
This moment in time was meant for me to be strong,
To find whatever entertainment that turned me on,
Under the big shade tree there goes I,
Watching the people as they pass by,
Some walking slow others in a hurry,
Some in deep thoughts others without worry,
Some with friends making plans for their day,
Other's alone going about their way,
Just moving on maybe with their families,
Talking fast as if they're rambling,
Wishing one would please notice me,
For I'm all alone under the big shade tree.

JACQUELINE JAMES

Falling Snow…

The fresh fallen snow drizzling down,
It chills the earth as it wets the ground,
Making it white for all eyes to see,
It's wet, and cold and about to freeze,
Now the temperature drops and it's a sheet of ice,
The snow continues to fall on top making 'sledding' nice,
It covers the earth like a blanket of mush,
To make the biggest snowman will be every kid's wish,
Everybody's having a snowball fights up and down the road,
With or without gloves they don't care if it's cold,
Everyone searches for the biggest hill to climb,
They'll have an awesome time reaching the top, while
they slip-and-slide,
Now they're coming down on their sleds full speed with a blast,
Wishing they could ride forever and the fun will forever last,
The schools closed because the roads are filled with snow,
But the parents are still driving and slipping-and-sliding because
they have places to go,
The trucks are coming to put salt on the road to melt up
all the snow,
It makes a mess and the cars are crashing and now they need a tow,
The sun comes out but it goes back in,
Now once more the snow freezes again,

INFINITY

Once again it covers the roads and it covers the cars,
It's winter my friends so don't drop your guards,
It's beautiful to watch the falling snow,
As I snuggle up by a cozy fire as it flow.

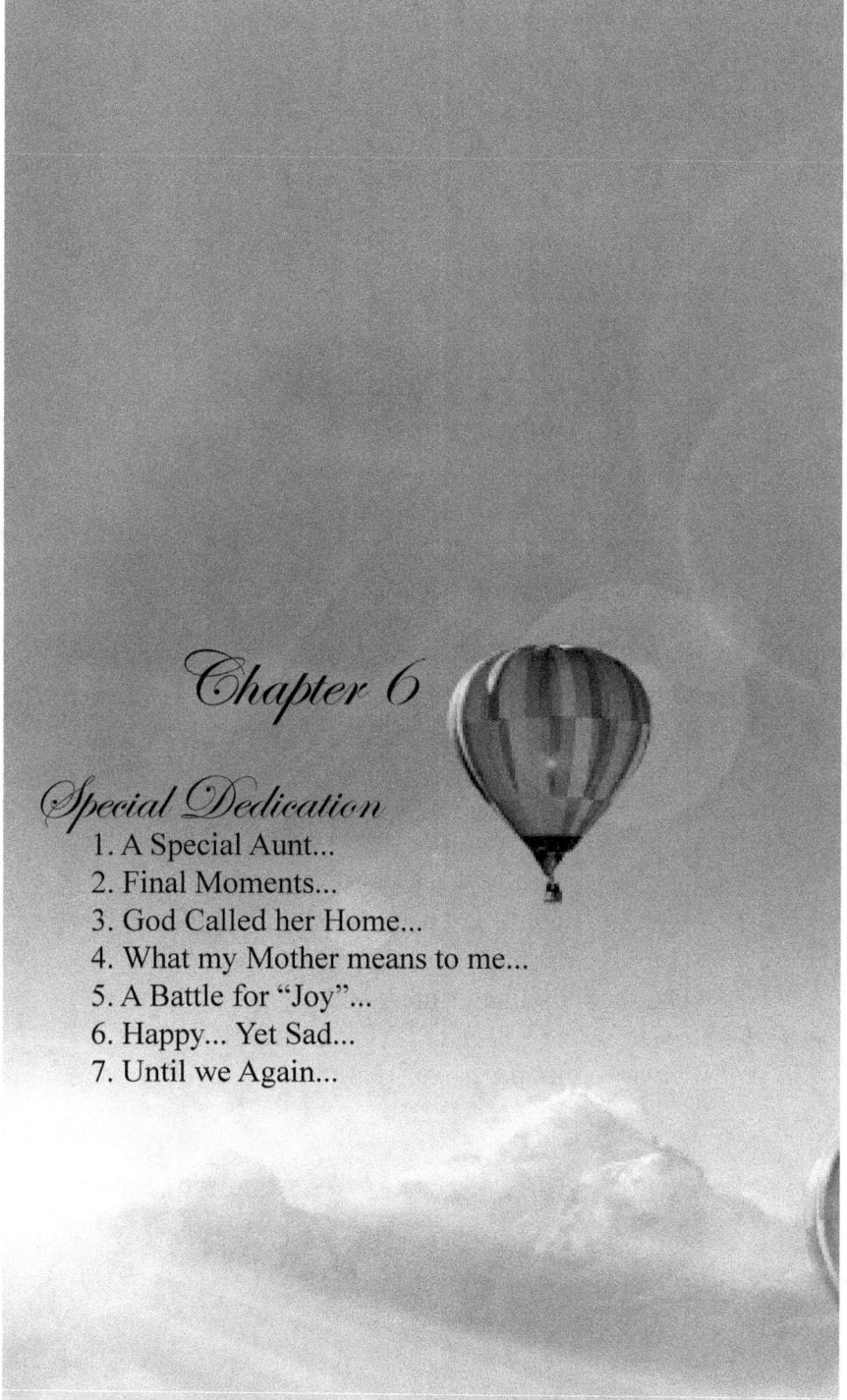

Chapter 6

Special Dedication

1. A Special Aunt...
2. Final Moments...
3. God Called her Home...
4. What my Mother means to me...
5. A Battle for "Joy"...
6. Happy... Yet Sad...
7. Until we Again...

INFINITY

Special Aunt...

So, you'll know what this poem is about,
I want you to know that you are my special aunt,
You're very precious and also dear,
Your very presence makes me cheer,
I'm glad you are an aunt of mine,
Cause, you're sweet, humble, and also kind,
You're wise beyond your years to come,
And you're always willing to show your love,
You're aging gracefully and that's for real,
Now it's time to sit back and chill,
You mean the world to me and you one of my favorites,
May God bless you for all of your labor,
I cherish the times we spent together,
The fun will stick in my heart like glue forever.
I love you dearly and that's for sure,
The feelings I have, are sincerely pure,
I'LL SCREAM IT LOUD I'LL ALSO SHOUT!
So you'll always remember you're my very special aunt!

Dedicated to					Loretta Smith

Jacqueline James

Final Moments...

My Aunt had been suffering for many day,
Because of the sickness in her body she could no longer stay,
During her final hours she refused to let go,
To leave her loves ones behind and give up the 'ghost',
We all believed that she held off for her granddaughter to come,
To feel for the last time that special love,
She started to aspirate and lose her manners,
We knew at that moment her body was shattered,
We prayed her life into the heavens,
We prayed until Our Lord and Savior would have her,
He ascended her soul into heaven above,
Because of God's mercy and Jesus loved,
I was blessed to be there to witness this event,
Her daughter's burdens were relieved, and their
minds were content,
We all felt a calm and sense of peace,
Because her pain had instantly ceased,
We gave God the glory as we lifted our hands,
Then, we all praise together with a victory dance,
We all felt 'Joy' because her situation was better,
She had going 'home' to live with the 'King' forever!
In Loving Memories:
Reatha Gene Whitehorn
(2-1-1945) – (7-27-2017)

INFINITY

God called her name...

July 27, 2017 @10:26pm Reatha Gene Whitehorn
was called home,
Our Lord and Savior accepted her spirit into the heavens,
We thank you Jesus for her life you've given,
God blessed her with some joyful days,
They were filled with love because she prayed,
God blessed her to be a loyal wife,
She's was mother of four beautiful children and had a
wonderful life,
She has very precious grandchildren who loves her so much,
They have blessed them with peace, in Jesus we trust,
She has a host of relatives, and friends, who loves her, and will
miss her as well,
Today we've come together to say our final fair wells,
God has carried her home to her special room,
Where she's at peace morning, night, and noon,
Her spirit is calm and she's able to rest,
Cause she's passed all of life's challenges and tests,
God was satisfied and her work here was complete,
So, He called her home for the 'Master' to meet.
She had to leave this heart-filled place,
In-order-to see 'Our Father's' face,
Yes, she left us all, but it's only temporary,
We'll meet her again there's no need to worry,

JACQUELINE JAMES

So, go ahead and mourn it's okay,
We'll feel her presence as we pray,
All though her body has departed,
Her spirit will always remain in our heart,
We thank you Jesus for calling her home,
Because of it our faith remains strong.

In Loving Memories:
Reatha Gene Whitehorn
(2-1-1946) - (7-27-17)

INFINITY

What my Mother means to me...

I'll always hold the highest respect for my mother,
For my mother was to entity, that transferred my life through God to this universe,
Her warm and sensitive presence is what I felt first,
She held the future of my life in her hands,
And she knew that love is what I demand,
Days to come and minutes to past,
She filled me up with a love after time past would last,
The joy I have is from the peace she brought,
When I think about how much I love my mother,
I hold that thought!
She's different from 'her' mom, or 'his',
For when I'm with my 'mom'- there isn't any other kids,
The selfish love I hold for her,
Is unlike any love one can compare,
There's not enough hours in time that's given,
To give all the love that I hold for her while I'm living,
It will extend beyond eternity and further,
For that's the destiny of love that I hold for my mother.

Jacqueline James

A Battle for Joy...

Lord Jesus it's hard,
Even though we all know that you're in charge,
Your perfect 'will-be-done' in every situation,
As we give you the 'glory', without hesitation,
You called 'home', my mother's first born child,
And, because of it she'll be heartbroken for a while,
However, God's a comforter in the mist of our storm,
We may weep and endure for a day but in the morning we'll find
'JOY'!
None of us here wanted her to go,
However, she was granted her 'wing' so she wouldn't have to
suffer anymore,
Her body was sick stricken with disease,
But she kept her 'faith', and for that God was pleased,
Yes, it's going to be hard cause she left two children behind to find
their way,
But, God will be with them each and every day,
And, her beautiful grandchildren who looked up to her for
guidance,
Just pray to 'Our Father', and they'll be able to find it,
For myself, our sister, and, our brother also,
We'll catch up with her later when it's our time to go,
For each, and every one of 'you', who love and cherished her,

INFINITY

Just look around please her memories are everywhere,
We thank you Jesus, because her battle was hard,
But, she fought all the way until she met the Lord!
Then, God gave her peace in mist of her storm!

In Loving Memories:
Joy Marie Thomas
(8-23-1960)-(9-20-2017)

JACQUELINE JAMES

Happy... Yet Sad...

I wanted to show some retrain with a bit of class,
But today my emotions were both happy and sad,
My oldest sister died which made me sad,
But thought of her being in heaven made my heart glad,
Today we put her body down into the dirt,
I know she's resting in heaven but it still really hurts,
Seeing all of my family and close friends made me smile,
But, the sorrow from our lost made us grieve for a while,
The way my siblings came together and comforted each other,
Made us appreciate that some of us were born through
different mothers,
Everyone was saddened with our hearts heavily weighed,
But, there was a sigh of relief at the end of the day,
The minister who delivered the eulogy touched all of our souls,
With the reassurance that God's in control,
He had to remind us that it was a 'home-going', service,
And through our faith God will relieve all of our burdens,
His perfect 'will' be done in every situation,
Allows us to understand why we were created,
We wept and endured on through the night,

INFINITY

But, our burdens were lighten by Jesus's light,
My heart was filled with pain piercing hard,
Then I found my 'peace', knowing she's gone with the 'Lord'!

In Loving Memories of:
                    Joy Marie Thomas
                    (8-23-60) - (9-20-17)

Jacqueline James

Until We Meet Again

For each of you I've left behind,
Filled with precious memories of my love you'll find,
Don't you dare cry for me,
I'm exactly where I need to be,
After a wonderful blessed journey God called me home,
I've earned my wings on my own,
God granted me to live a righteous life,
As a daughter, a mother, a sister, a cousin, a friend, and as a wife,
However my days on earth as of now has ceased,
I'm with my Lord and Savior in prefect peace,
There's so many rooms and mine was reserved,
God said "Well done my good and faithful servant this is what you deserve"!
He relieved me from my pain and suffering,
Into His arms a place of comfort,
I know that you all miss me but it's okay,
We'll meet again on God's scheduled day,
Everything is prepared through God's extraordinary design,
Take care of each other until that time,
God will extend His mercy and His grace,
Then you will also be blessed to see His face!
In Loving memories: Evelyn Hollowell

Sunrise May 1, 1945
Sunset July 3, 2020

INFINITY

www.ingramcontent.com/pod-product-compliance
Lightning Source LLC
Chambersburg PA
CBHW070433010526
44118CB00014B/2027